City

City AN ESSAY

Brian Lennon

The University of Georgia Press

ATHENS & LONDON

Paperback edition, 2011

© 2002 by the University of Georgia Press

Athens, Georgia 30602

www.ugapress.org

Printed digitally in the United States of America

The Library of Congress has cataloged the hardcover edition of
this book as follows:
Library of Congress Cataloging-in-Publication Data
LCCN Permalink: http://lccn.loc.gov/2001045114

Lennon, Brian, 1971–
    City : an essay / Brian Lennon.
        100 p. ; 22 cm.
    ISBN 0-8203-2321-7 (alk. paper)
    "Winner of the Associated Writing Programs award for
creative nonfiction."
    Includes bibliographical references.
    1. City and town life.
    2. New York (N.Y.) I. Title.
    PS3612.E54 C5   2002
    814'.6 21   20-1045114

PAPERBACK ISBN-13: 978-0-8203-4103-3
ISBN-10: 0-8203-4103-7

British Library Cataloging-in-Publication Data available

Portions of this work appeared previously, often in different
form, in the journals *Conjunctions, Fence, The Gettysburg Review,
The Iowa Review, 100 Words,* and *Seneca Review.*

Cover photographts by Kristan Lennon
Cover design based on the original by Erin Kirk New

Language shows clearly that memory is not an instrument for exploring the past but its theater. It is the medium of past experience, as the ground is the medium in which dead cities lie interred.

—Walter Benjamin

Contents

I » BROADWAY

BROADWAY—the expectant tongue of a communicant. Red taillight waves: s-shapes bobbing on an asphalt sea; streaking, bleeding it. There was a late night TV advertisement, a time lapse film of Broadway traffic: just *lights,* surging in double time, as the sun sank and rose over the City. I couldn't sleep without TV. West End Avenue began beneath my window, which looked out on a marquee, a bar, a grocery; a skyline out of Fritz Lang. My mother and sister visited, brought flowers. So small! You're lucky you don't need *things.* The street hummed outside: *Broadway.* Mnemonic vectors. A park. Light striping over the walls at night; roar of a bus, impatient car horn; voices. Voices, in an ambient *Mrm mrm mrm.* Or occasionally: *Fuck you! Help!* and the recursive scuffling of feet.

ON THE WET STREET yellow taxis are boxy ghosts; are iridescent smears; are gnat-clouds or cones of electric rain. Umbrellas, and here and there a newspaper, a hood, a haughtily or exultantly wet head. But nearly everyone has black umbrellas. . . . *Viewed from above:* they form a river of dark stars, flowing in both directions. And people hurry in the rain: the long yanked arcs of the umbrellas tell you that; the bob and weave; the clip on a crowded stretch, when the weaker held one revolves—see it now—round a chrome spine; a curse, a rushed apology. To the City sounds add *sssssssssssss:* a drowning static; droplets lisping on the tar; sprayed out behind the tires of a taxi, a speeding bus. *Near the fruit bins of the grocery:* a figure blinks through sheets of water; clutches a greasy coin-filled cup. *A wet dog:* barks where it has been—forgotten?—tied to a meter outside a restaurant.

ELUDING THE TENTACLES OF BOSS TWEED, Alfred Ely Beach constructs his experimental "pneumatic subway" in secret, renting the basement of a clothing store on lower Broadway and tunneling under the block between Murray and Warren Streets at night. Unveiled in 1871, his demonstration track and station includes a waiting room with frescoes, a fountain, a goldfish tank, and a grand piano. When Tweed is indicted, Beach is granted a city subway charter by Governor John Dix, but public enthusiasm for the project wanes and Beach is unable to raise the money to proceed. *The block-long tube:* sealed—to be forgotten until 1912, when subway construction crews tunneling under Broadway break through the wall of Beach's waiting room, its appointments entirely intact.

INSIDE, LOOPING BLUE WAVES: a saxophone floats over a piano, somewhere behind the cymbal's tick: the speech of the moon, of Night, of warmly lit windows in tall buildings. I stand at the window in a rhombus of refracted light, recall a friend's advice: *To hear music as conversation.* Down on the street, two figures embrace beneath umbrellas; the dog sniffs at their shoes; the figure clutching the cup asks them *for change.* The blue notes are prickling on my neck. I want a drug to draw the music into me, to wash it through—rain sluicing in the street, transfusion. Down on the street. Down on the street, two figures embrace beneath umbrellas; a dog sniffs at their shoes; a figure clutching a cup asks them *for change—*

DOWN ON THE STREET at six o'clock: a chill fall evening. A pulsing sun sinks into the silhouetted jaw of the apartment blocks across the Hudson; small planes glide upriver, wing lights winking. I am walking south, through swirls and eddies of newspaper and dust, through the bag-carrying crowd. Tractor-trailers, buses, yellow taxis and private cars, cyclists and skaters barrel and jostle down the stretch; the restaurants and bars are filling; under the fading purple sky they throw their magical, inviting, incandescent human light onto the sidewalk; and carpet Broadway with it. There is nothing quite so assuring as these tableaux of figures eating: in talking laughing groups; in quiet pairs; in intense, contented solitude opposite a propped-up book. —And waiting outside, others are rattling coin-filled cups—

IN 1850 THE UPPER WEST SIDE is an open area of small farms, shantytowns and country houses. *A photograph taken in 1862:* two men on a dirt path lined with hedges and trees, branches bowering overhead; more a lane than a thoroughfare. *The Bloomingdale Road:* is widened in 1868 and renamed the Boulevard; but public transportation is still limited to one loop of the Eighth Avenue streetcar, which runs as far north as Eighty-fourth Street. In 1880 service begins on the Ninth Avenue El, and a few years later the *Times* reports: "The west side of the city presents just now a scene of building activity such as was never before witnessed. . . . The huge masses of rock which formerly met the eye, usually crowned by a rickety shanty and a browsing goat, are being blasted out of existence."

I HAVE EXITED MY BUILDING; crossed through the park; across 106th Street, dodging a bus, walking more quickly; weaving through students in front of Augie's; heading for 96th Street and beyond. *The site of a farmhouse where Poe once lived:* "As late as 1893, there stood on a height of rock on the south side of Eighty-fourth Street east of the Boulevard, where the cutting through of the street had left it, an old colonial house, once the residence of Edgar Allan Poe. . . . In the olden time . . . the house commanded a magnificent view both up and down the Hudson." Difficult to see—here where any spot on the street commands a magnificent view of . . . *itself—*

BEFORE THIS FALL EVENING, before all fall evenings to come . . .
I had been living without breathing, without catching breath. The
work now was excavation. Perhaps that's why I didn't walk much at
first, out on the Great Public Road, *but watched it from my window
instead—*

AFTER PEARL HARBOR U.S. troop ships returning to New York carried for ballast rubble from the bombed city of Bristol; this rubble—remnants of homes—was used as landfill in the construction of a portion of East River Drive, afterward named Bristol Basin. *A message:* tells the adventure of *that* matter: raised out of the earth by human hands, used to build homes; destroyed by others; transported over an ocean, dumped into a river to make land to build a road on—

AND ON THIS FALL EVENING I am unable to find the message on Poe's house; at Eighty-fourth Street, a very loud argument pits a newsstand vendor against a figure in a parka; the parka's filling is falling out as they jump and wave their arms. I cross the street, it continues; a crowd gathers; epithets fly; the City police cruise up. It is half cold, the sun only a faint glow in the cross streets. I decide I only half care about Poe's house. I go into an unpleasantly sparkling coffee bar and sit at the window, pressing the paper cup between my palms—

ON THIS FALL EVENING. I went for a walk, to find the message.
I couldn't find it; I only half cared; I sat in the window of a coffee
bar. It was six-thirty on a fall evening, on Broadway, in my life. I
would like to say I walked the streets all night, or rode the trains,
on this fall evening; but I did not. I went into a bar instead. *When
I emerged:* the pavement glittered; I thought, "I am glad to be
alive." Mnemonics select the scene framed in the window at sun-
rise, when I returned home: a sky hemmed pink and blue, hanging
in strips between the buildings, traversed by a small plane; the
squatting water tanks in silhouette; the still-illumined windows
of others who had not yet yielded to sleep. There was a moment
of suspension, as of a collective holding of the breath; and then
outside Broadway came to life again: car horns, air brakes, voices
rebounded in its canyons—

II » SLEEP

AT FIRST THINGS COLLIDE, collude, drive you along. Only later do they begin to "fall apart." You move in a kind of trance, the blind trust that day after day brings somehow usable experience, and that even if you are only waiting, something is bound to happen that will clarify just what was all along at stake. But it is a privilege to speak of one's experience as though it were unique, not quotidian, not irreducibly ordinary. In complex moments when my window frames an indigo dawn, or the lunch-hour inferno, or a sunset of profound silhouettes, nothing can be further from the truth. The pageantry of Broadway furnishes proof: fistfights, arguments, embraces, self-conscious posturing of all kinds; the way people walk or set their mouths when they feel threatened, or angry; favor and petition flickering on faces. Those silhouettes. "Blank windows gargle signals through the roar" (Crane).

UNDER THE GROUND of the self, too, there is a system: lanterns and signs, spelling out something. What? Regret, ambition, hope, despair; wreckage and splintering and boredom. And other, happier, more wholesome modes and tropes. For the others, mnemonics constructs a composite, surface image: heart's photograph. In this picture, boxy yellow taxis glide serenely through the midday autumn mist; a theater marquee, right center, is missing letters; yellow light floods through the glass doors onto the pavement. A figure stands there, pondering. The marquee is pitched just slightly over her head. The film is entitled *Sleep*.

THE MYSTERY OF LIVES, recursively in how many waves, a near-infinity of ghosts: concentration of the City. In the hour between 3 and 4 A.M., when it breathes in an equilibrium of surge and repose, you can hear something like the footsteps of the dead—

ATTEMPTING THE CONCEPTION of a diagram of one's own life. Key information might be represented as on the map of an old city, with its center, its concentric rings. Here and there might be marked—with pins, or flags—the homes of friends and lovers, the place of one's birth, schools one attended; this map would, presumably, link up with others, representing the essence of one's life, the vitals of its location, and perhaps its flow—much as one might, from the précis of a book, construct a chart of the arguments.

"I" SITS LOOKING OUT over the street. It is noisy and brightly lit. "I" watches traffic accidents during the day, brawls outside Cannon's at night. From the chair at my desk "I" looks down a thorough-fare—Upper Broadway—that vanishes, foreshortened, as yellow taxis stream into points of light.

AN AMBULANCE TURNS into side streets, disappears, emerges—
lost?—then, almost calmly, grinds over the median: one front wheel
dangling, trailing shards. A figure gets out, looks doubtfully around,
throws up its hands, sits on a trash can, lights a cigarette. It is snow-
ing. The figure throws up its hands again. *You* are passing—dressed
in black; quickly turning white.

PERHAPS THE CITY, always erasing and being erased, renders the notion of "origin" absurd; and yet there is a sanctity that sticks to *place,* as we know when we recall the apartments and restaurants, the park benches and public telephones, long since claimed by others, that once were accessories of our own—

FIRE IS THERE or it is not there. Look! my child-brother said slicing his finger through the candle flame, It doesn't hurt.—But surely there is a word for that moment when a fire log, beneath its bark, has become one immanent ember, winking like a City or a circuit board; for that moment when you know only the desire, no, the *need* to *stir it up*. What is on fire, you ask yourself, staring into that waiting. What is that moment. What is the word?

III » NOTES TO THE UNWRITTEN

[1]fording

STRESSED HERE IS THE "FORDING"—i.e., striving toward continuity—enacted by the *reader,* on whom as much responsibility rests as on the writer. As a child, I waited with my mother for my father, returning by train from the school in the City. Kneeling on the seat of the car, viewing the illumined platform, I knew that we— my mother, my father, and me—formed a unit that divided and combined each day, and that this was an arrangement of some consequence. I had no understanding—that came later—but I had impressions.

²loss

THE CHARACTER AND PROPORTION of "loss" differs among the bereaved (the taken-from, the robbed). For example: A, pulling her jeans on, catches a toe in the hole worn through one knee. The small hole becomes a large one. A is overjoyed: an unforced disaster lends her a rakish air. B, performing the same action, suffers chagrin: now his knee will be exposed to drafts, etc.

³participation mystique

HERE, I SUPPOSE, I AM TOYING with the notion of *participation mystique:* "imaginative identification with people and objects outside oneself, regarded as an attribute of primitive peoples by the French anthropologist Lucien Lévy-Bruel (1857–1939); merging of the individual consciousness with that of a group or with the external world. 1966 j. b. priestly *Moments* 228 In our early childhood . . . we exist in a state that a French anthropologist has called *participation mystique*" (*OED*). For me, the object was the City. My father raced into it every day, returning exhausted, a Jonah with a briefcase. We picked him up. My mother drove us home. After dinner, I dreamed of trains.

[4]truth

STATED ANOTHER WAY: "because" is *as real as a blank look*. On these magically dark evenings, I had a feeling of immersion, of participation in the greater world—a "taking place," providing the link between my father's train and our home—that delighted me obscurely, and which still makes riding out to the airport for someone I love (especially at night) inexplicably enjoyable. *Inexplicably*, because I don't know what I relish more: the meeting, or the velvet solitude of its approach.

[5]lonely

ALTHOUGH THE TWO are usually designated "estrangement" and "integration," other vocabularies are useful. You don't always know, for instance, that you are lonely. You may feel *free*, or *stoical*, or *intrepid*.

[6]waking dreams

DURRELL—OTHERWISE, A PIG—knew this perfectly. E.g., *Justine:*
"At this time he had already begun to experience that great cycle of
historical dreams which now replaced the dreams of his childhood
in his mind, and into which the City now threw itself—as if at last
it had found a responsive subject through which to express the collective desires, the collective wishes, which informed its culture. . . .
These disturbed him for they were not at all the dreams of the
night-hours. They overlapped reality and interrupted his waking
mind as if the membrane of his consciousness had been suddenly
torn in places to admit them."

[7]summer

THIS BLOCK OF 256TH STREET: sunny; treeless, but lawned; lined with houses raised on foundations; chain-link fences boxing in the yards. *Children:* everywhere—on bicycles, on roller skates, on Big Wheels, on hands and knees. *In summer:* we splashed in tiny plastic pools; mothers on beach chairs reading magazines; the ice cream truck tinkling a melancholy "Ode to Joy."

[8]repetition

I CONFESS THAT I HAVE NO IDEA what Kierkegaard (or his persona, Constantin Constantius) meant by "repetition." Here, however, I mean to say that successive iterations of one single event multiply its existing points of entry. *I was born:* on the eastmost fringe of the City, in an enclave at the foot of the airport, and I learned to sleep through the scream of jets, which I knew traveled over the ocean. *My earliest awareness of the City:* at the station, where I waited with my mother, in the idling car, for my father. *At one end of the block:* "the creek"—a tract of spongy undeveloped land, beyond which stretched the runways. *From the creek:* the frogs that filled our yards; Gina Ragazza, two doors down, pressed sharpened sticks through their bodies—twitch, twitch—as airliners floated roaring overhead.

[9]falling

Cf. HEIDEGGER, SEIN UND ZEIT, ¶38: "The phenomenon of falling does not give us something like a 'night view' of being. . . . Far from determining its nocturnal side, it constitutes all being's days in their everydayness." A depressing thought, if you are an optimist; otherwise, consolation?

[10]sleeping

A SOMEWHAT MORE EXPANSIVE formula has been offered by Nietz-schenstein: "What we cannot speak about, we may nonetheless utter through a mask." This happens all the time. For example: "I have never been so lonely in my whole life." Or: "Your friend is *sleeping*."

IV » TEXT ON THE WEATHER

lets go to the other meeeeteeeeooooorooooloooogies

—TRISTAN TZARA

IN MY DREAMS I AM A WEATHER-MAN on TV. I originate in this medium, it feels right, it pits me against the vicissitudes of life. When the call comes to rouse the City-dwellers from their slumbers it is not too soon to dream of love, the hot filaments of its success. That is what fills me.

I say "originate" to counter your objection that nothing can originate, that all is flux and loop and cycle, that there is no alpha and omega, that there is no line along which you drag your life saying "Now I'm getting somewhere, now I'm getting there." I say "medium" to counter your objection that I pretend, that I am faking it, that I am giving you nothing, that I am being hysterical. The threshold of my house is not hysteria. There is nothing in the weather I can control. I am all corners, you cannot get to me.

To know the weather is to know that you are helpless, not to lose hope. . . .

INTERVIEW WITH THE SUCCESSFUL WEATHER-MAN

Tell us how you became etc etc etc

I was all jammed up. Unmotivated. I had a complacent office job where mostly I did the crosswords. One day the boss went on a rampage and by sundown I was the only one left employed.

What happened then

I was jobless. There is nothing better, until you begin to starve. I had to find a hustle. An acquaintance told me she had supported herself for a year by playing darts in City bars. Beating drunken macho men out of twenty, thirty, fifty bucks.

Oh how interesting could you elaborate

It sounded good to me. I dislike drunken macho men. I like bars. I thought: I'll move to the City, take up darts.

And then

(The Successful Weather-Man sprints from the room)

TERMINOLOGY: 1. hysteria: The more or less total loss of emotional control. [The term is from the smug sequences of male-dominant thinking. Greek males, priding themselves on their emotional steadiness, ascribed loss of emotional control to the behavior of women. Concluding that it stemmed from the malfunctioning of some organ specific to women, they imagined they had located the source in *hustera*, the womb, whence *husterikos*, of the (malfunctioning) womb.] 2. gestalt modification: The alteration of an unusual word form into one more or less approximating it but more familiar. See *galleywest, hangnail, sea cook*. 3. bellot: Winds blowing through the narrow Strait of Bellot, connecting the Gulf of Boothia and Franklin Strait in the Canadian high arctic.

AXIOMS; POSSIBLE OR PROBABLE SLOGANS:

1. Weather is unpredictable and cannot be forecast.
2. Hurricane Hunters fly into the eye of the storm.
3. Blizzards are the most dramatic and perilous of winter storms.
4. True or false: you are safe from a tornado in your basement.
5. One of the surprise products of a hot summer afternoon thunderstorm is the almost magical transformation of the landscape from verdant green to icy white with the onset of a hailstorm.
6. Photographs taken from space enable one to see and interpret a wide range of meteorological phenomena.
7. In less enlightened times primitive peoples assigned animistic roles to weather phenomena such as the waterspout, dust devil (haboob), et al.
8. We are living in more enlightened times.

POSSIBLE OR PROBABLE NARRATIVES:

1. Girl meets boy; weather ensues.
2. Girl, boy, and small dog are separated from home by giant tornado.
3. Girl fails to make it in publishing, resolves to have a go at meteorology.
4. Girl appears as forecaster on the local news. Friends celebrate; family sobs.
5. Girl becomes nationally famous Weather-Man. However, Weather-Map persistently malfunctions on the eleven o'clock wrap-up, making Girl an object of persistent ridicule. Family sobs more heartily.
6. Girl, nursing heartache, converts to a wholly positivistic world view, resolving never to permit anything from occurring unforeseen, "ever again."

MEDITATIVE OPENINGS FOR A TEXT ON THE WEATHER:

1. As long as I can remember I have been fascinated by the weather, etc.
2. More than ten years ago, I drove through bad weather, etc.
3. It is ten years ago. I drive through bad weather, etc.
4. Toward the end of a spell of especially inclement weather, etc.
5. Love is weather—, etc.
6. O, the Weather!

NOTES TOWARD AN ESSAY ON THE WEATHER:

stratus undulatus: as though what went softly piling over the land were nothing more than fluffy clouds

stratus translucidus: as in a photograph you once made in a valley north of Rome

stratus opacus nebulosus: as over the City, on one of those days when you never once unclench your teeth

stratus opacus uniformis: as when silence fills your apartment overnight

NOTES TOWARD AN ESSAY ON THE WEATHER:

Notes toward Intentions

» To ensure that readers of the Essay do not attempt to comprehend the Weather.
» To encourage them to acquire their own Instruments.
» To arrange things so that Weather speaks for itself.

Notes toward Procedures

» To choose the proper cloud formations.
» To arrange for geographically lucid winds.
» To articulate clearly the threat of disaster.

NOTES TOWARD AN ESSAY ON THE WEATHER:

The two principal approaches to the Weather:

1. At all costs to endure the Weather, even when the Weather takes over, and runs, and ruins, and wrecks, and wracks. At all costs to court the Calm in the Eye of the Storm. If possible to fly like a Hurricane Hunter into the Eye of the Storm.

2. To follow the Bellot, or other winds, viz., the Chinook, the Chocolatero, the Collada, the Coromell, the Easter, the Palouser, the Sonora, the Washoe Zephyr, where they may take you.

EXPLICATION

The more or less total loss of emotional control. As in: AAAAAAAAAAAAAAAAAAAAAAAAAAAAAAAAAAAAAAAAAAAAA!

In my dreams I am a Weather-Man on TV. The subject, a demented rationalist, longs simultaneously for the social utility of life-saving predictions and the wholly selfish glory of their success.

I'll move to the City, take up darts. . . . Clearly the Successful Weather-Man never made it to the City.

Girl fails to make it in publishing. . . . This assumes that Girl had in fact attempted to "make it" in publishing.

More than ten years ago: Refers to a specific time in the life of the Successful Weather-Man.

ENCOUNTER BETWEEN THE SUCCESSFUL WEATHER-MAN
AND A HABOOB

SUCCESSFUL WEATHER-MAN: Out, out!

(haboob slinks away)

NOTES TOWARD AN ESSAY ON THE WEATHER:

To make clear that there is nothing one can "do about" the Weather. The Weather is given. The Weather is not to be "improved." The Weather may be critiqued, as in: God-damn this Weather! But it cannot be influenced.

At the same time to make clear that it is "the meaning of our lives" that we may critique the weather. Without this, what would we do? Simply live under it, like cats.

INTERVIEW WITH THE SUCCESSFUL WEATHER-MAN

What are the so to speak larger issues etc. we're dealing with here

Moonbow aurora parhelia halo of 22°

Do you believe that you can read the future in the sky

The sky overhead is nature's canvas

Do you ever feel that your task is hopeless

The medical term for snow blindness is niphablepsia

V » LOVE IS THREE THINGS

I can escape from the world I see by giving up attack thoughts.

LOVE IS LETTING GO of fear. Or is it fear's embrace? More ut-
terly—this is awkward, I know—than before. No. Love is a colored
pattern board. . . . No. Love is a mosaic. I have a weakness for narration, she told me one night as I boarded a flight to the City. I
think—she said—this is related to the fear of death, what do you
think? But I am a nervous flyer and was thinking about vertigo.
Later, watching the plane's shadow skim a quilt of clouds, I thought
about it and I decided she was right: narration is about the fear of
death. As you guard yourself you turn the page. . . . What happens
next? But you are already there, already *past* there. So love is letting
go of fear, of the fear of not knowing what happens next. Or is it
fear's embrace? More completely—this is awkward, I know—than
before. No. Love is a colored pattern board, by which I mean it
gives you the chance to match *your blue* to *someone else's red—*

OF COURSE, HAVING THE CHANCE is little more than having the chance. The most strenuous of us do nothing with it. Rilke is known best for dwelling on this:

> Bilden die Nächte sich nicht aus dem schmerzlichen Raum
> aller der Arme die jäh ein Geliebter verließ.

> Aren't nights built of the pained space
> of all embraces that a lover suddenly lost.

Did Rilke try, in the sense that is meant when we say "Try to love me" or "Try to forget me"? Well, yes and no. He tried to live sincerely but ended by making himself unbearable. A not uncommon outcome. So love is a colored pattern board, on which ready symmetries lay waiting; and yet knowing them is another thing—

This instant is the only time there is.

LOVE IS FINDING BALANCE. Or is it balance's loss? More totally—
this is awkward, I know—than before. No. Love is a still life. No.
Love is a nude. I have a weakness for word processing. Perhaps
this is also about the fear of death. What do you think? she said.
But I am a nervous lover and was thinking about the Kierkegaard-
ian malaise. Later, as the City lit up like a circuit board beneath
the wing, I thought about it and I decided: Word processing is
about the fear of death. As you stare into the screen you sidestep
time. . . . But you are still in time, are always in time. So love is
finding balance, a balance of time wasted and well spent. Or is it
balance's loss? More catastrophically—this is awkward, I know—
than before. No. Love is a still life, by which I mean it suspends
time—

OF COURSE, SUSPENDING TIME is little more than suspending time. The most directed of us do nothing with it. Birdwatchers are known best for dwelling on this:

The Three Great Secrets of Birdwatching
1. It is what it appears to be!
2. What you don't see is as important as what you do see.
3. Before you look, know what you're looking for.

Do birdwatchers find balance, in the sense that is meant when we say "You make me lose my balance" or "You balance me"? Well, yes and no. Typically they have one foot in life and one in a book. A not uncommon situation. So love is a still life, in which something seems *about to stir;* and yet it *mustn't stir.* No. Love is a nude that you paint and you pose for in turn—

The past is over—it can touch me not.

LOVE IS WHAT YOU make it. Or is it what you find? More success-
fully—this is awkward, I know—than before. No. Love is keen
competition for 2, 3 or 4 players. No. Love is America's favorite
family game. I have a weakness for the nude of you, I told my
lover. Is that about the fear of death? she asked. But I am a nervous
painter and was thinking about the moment when the sitter says,
"May I see?" Later, when I called her from the apartment in the
City, I said "I have thought about it and my weakness for the nude
of you is about the fear of death." So love is what you make it,
what you build it with. Or is it what you find? More ecstatically—
this is awkward, I know—than before. No. Love is keen competition for 2, 3, or 4 players, by which I mean that in it you confront
yourself—

OF COURSE, TO CONFRONT yourself is little more than to confront yourself. The most stoical of us do little with it. Frank Hardy, of The Hardy Boys, is known best for dwelling on this:

Frank fought down a surge of panic. He had wriggled some distance away from the eaves. Now he must work his way back and try to overcome his assailant before the man could pull his gun.

Is Frank a hero, in the sense that is meant when we say "You are my hero" or "We don't need another hero"? Well, yes and no. He plays the gallant but has no time for voyeurs—his work comes first. A not uncommon preference. So love is keen competition for 2, 3, or 4 players, in which you have wriggled some distance from the eaves. . . . No. Love is America's favorite family game. It begins in the nude of you. It is your narration—

VI » NINETEEN ITALIAN DAYS

1.1 FOR THE TRAVELERS, the essay begins on a plane: a plane towing its shadow over a cloud, then slicing into it (inside the plane, this is like the rush of a mood: abruptly *elsewhere*) and sinking while mist breathes past the windows, swirls in the jets; a plane creaking and yawing over Chicago, en route to New York, en route to Rome; a plane invaded by the yellow midwinter light pouring through a sliced-through cloud, which makes the travelers feel, for once, like travelers in a photograph in the in-flight magazine, the timelessness of which suggests . . . well, timelessness; a plane that fails to plunge or to explode, a plane that instead of plunging or exploding lands in a City of bridges-like-blue-skeletons, a City in which telephones are located and used—an act which, for the writers, marks the beginning of the essay;

I.2—THROUGH THIS CITY, in which, for the writers, the essay begins, there walk the travelers—who are on their way to Rome, another city, in which another essay will begin, in which, perhaps, the essay will truly and finally begin: for who is to say where what begins, perhaps the essay truly begins in Rome, and the essay that begins on the plane over Chicago, the essay that begins in New York, are impostor essays; perhaps we need to slice through the impostor essays to the real ones: in any case, the travelers, having used telephones, walk through the City, which was, and still is, home;

1.3—NOW THEY THINK BACK to the plane rising over a cornfield of stacked clouds and strings of sun and sprinklers and distant pickups trailing dust; now they think back to the plane landing in a City of bridges-like-blue-skeletons; now they turn left, now right, now right again, mnemonics; now they ascend the stairs to an apartment; now they enter the apartment; they stay a while, then the travelers and the writers leave the apartment, they retrace their steps, they locate telephones, they board a plane, they sit for seven hours in cramped seats in the darkness and the light until finally they arrive in Rome, which is where the essay—for the travelers? for the writers?—begins. . . .

2.1 CELLINI WAS THE NORMAN MAILER of the Italian Renaissance. He punches Michelangelo in the nose. He jumps out a window to attack a rival with a dinner knife. He admits to the assassination of at least three innocent men. His life is a series of scrapes with hot-blooded Spaniards, beastly Frenchmen, rascally priests, choleric bishops, insane jailers, and capricious popes, all of whom he outwits with ease. He survives being poisoned with a powdered diamond and being struck in the chest by a chunk of castle during the sack of Rome. ("I came to life again by the means of more than twenty leeches applied to my buttocks," he writes of that incident.)

2.2 I WONDER IF NORMAN MAILER ever read Cellini. On the highway north of Rome, a statue of the Virgin Mary leans up into a clear blue sky, unusual (they say) in January. Behind her the trail of a jet spreads, flattens, floats away. Like the fog this morning over the runway; like breath. On the horizon, mountains like overlapping felt. Headlamps gliding along the *strada bianca* far below.

2.3 HAIRPIN TURNS and a steep grade: the rented Golf snarls and stalls in the gravel as we wait for a woodcutter's truck to lumber by. Ears pop during the climb; two of the four of us are nauseous: "Mmmh." Then, weeds tick along the panels beneath our feet, we crest the mountain into a cleared space, on one rim of which there squats the house.

All my love's in vain, someone in the back sings, sickly.

But isn't this a view. To the west, the sun flinging blood and taffeta across the sky; a line of clouds advancing. The stone house with seven chimneys and the sunset banging off the panes. And a woodpile, and a cat with a pushed-in face.

3.1 HOW DO YOU CROSS THE STREET in the City? And other speculations. Language swelling like water or come drilling at you. The Golf's engine on these roads. In the headlights, skin of the landscape: valley shadow. And one particular road sign.

Stringed light traces the tower. Darkened houses ringing the piazza: below, on the stones, your steps ring and the different and same night bursts on your eyes.

3.2 "IF I WERE TO DESCRIBE all the wonderful things that happened to me up to this time," Cellini writes, "and all the great dangers to my own life which I ran, I should astound my readers." He is a study in promised restraint that fails. How do you stop telling stories, so you can live? How do you stop promising? These are questions for the writer.

For the traveler there are other, more pressing questions. *Dov'è il gabinetto* (Where is the toilet)? *Dov'è il cuore* (Where is the heart)?

4.1 LIGHT PLANES IN RHOMBOIDS from the facades, flutters down onto the head like cloth. Not hard to see how Tuscany produced the painters. And we are here, at the Museo Civico, Sansepolcro, to visit one: Piero della Francesca, whose heavy-eyed Madonna *della Misericordia* and rising Christ are modestly roped off in a bare room. (And a relaxed Sebastian, enduring his arrows.)

"Look at their feet," you say.

4.2 AT THE SHRINE of the Madonna *del Parto,* Monterchi, which includes an exhibit detailing the painting's restoration, I agree that Piero neglected feet.

5.1 GRAPPA MAKES US so quickly drunk, we can't believe our luck. We stumble from the café into the piazza relieved, for a few moments, of our shadows. *Is it good to say, Sit down, I will take it to you?*

5.2 BEYOND ETRUSCAN AND ROMAN WALLS, on a hillside, a small fire drifts smoke. A cloud pushes over the terraces of vines; somewhere deep in Cortona bells bong.

6.1 A CAT SITS IN A PORTICO in the amphitheater of the Boboli Gardens. A section of light glides over the lawn; the cat melts into it. After a banker quarried stone here for his *palazzo* the crater was made into a stage for opera. And then . . . Luca Pitti, the banker, went bankrupt. Hubris and building costs had done him in. Ironically, a guidebook notes, Palazzo Pitti was purchased by the Medici, whom Pitti had been trying to outbuild in the first place. *They* used the stage for jousts and (hm) naval battles.

6.2 A GOOD TRAVEL GUIDE, like a good cookbook, is pugnacious. This one sneers and steams ("a Mannerist folly . . .") and we are half in love with it. But it is nineteen years out of date. Of the amphitheater, it notes: "part of an Egyptian obelisk"; "in the niches, terracotta urns. . . ." Where now, in the first place, there is a gigantic basin under a scaffold (only the feet protrude); where in the second place there are only cats.

The sun: a sheet over the lawn. The Duomo: a pastry. The guidebook sneering; the frozen cats; statues twitching at the edge of the frame. We sit on a stone bench near a yawning god, compose ourselves. Or rather: we are decomposed. . . .

7.1 A CAT SITS IN A PORTICO in the amphitheater of the Boboli Gardens. In the photograph it is a black speck with ears, just barely visible above the—sill? lip? rim?—of the cornice. Behind it rises the trough intended for the urn; above that, a fanlike ornament; then a triangular crown. Below, decaying stone stairs; behind, a box hedge and some wild trees, which from this angle look like they're blowing straight up in the air. Now that I look again I see its tail: a third point there, beside the ears.

7.2 AT NIGHT, STATUES in darkness. Coins of cats' eyes. Stone and fur-flesh against the sky . . . what does it mean to *tell them apart?*

It *does* light up at night, like a real City. Down there at the foot of the hill, electricity winds shabbily through alleys; the spires and the burdened bridge *too* old. And on the hilltops to the south, towns glitter like isolated humming brains. We walk. At the end of the Viottolone, Perseus charges through a still pond under the moon, stone cape streaming out behind. "Makes my toes curl," you say. Recline on a stone bench. Sleep . . .

8 AFTER THE EARTHQUAKES, entire streets are braced on both sides by scaffolds: a City of tunnels, like a mine. Even the tiny house windows are biting down on wooden props. And fog hangs over Assisi like something alive: can't see to the ends of the streets. On the piazza, a fountain in sections, melting and vanishing.

The photograph is a photograph of fog. Our backs turned to the lens; lines of the piazza's stones rush past us. Dimly, in the upper left corner, columns of the Tempio di Minerva.

9.1 IN 217 B.C., AT LAGO TRASIMENO, 16,000 Roman soldiers are slaughtered by Hannibal's army, which ran them down these mountains into the lake. That stretch of beach, from which battle remains are still being recovered, is bracketed by Sanguineto (the Place of Blood) and Ossaia (the Place of Bones).

What mountains? Guidebook abandoned: I thought I wanted to escape maps and names.

Not so.

Shoes popping and sucking in the mud.

Humid; I loosen my scarf.

9.2 THIS MUD: is it *sand?* Red-yellow . . . Rainwater in tire tracks, footprints.

Trees and shrubs closing (what kind of tree, what kind of shrub?); a clearing, air; the house; the valley, a tiny church, a car creeping along the road.

Shoes sinking into mud. I am too warm. Warm body air pouring from collar.

A clearing. A ruined castle on the ridge opposite, walls gnawing the sky.

Church bells. Wild pig tracks. Oak trees?

Picking up kindling.

9.3 OUR NEIGHBOR IS NAMED DANTE, is not Italian, is from Chicago. Listens to the third movement of the Third Symphony each afternoon. At night we dim the lights, set to flailing and choking on the fire. Logs hissing and foaming yesterday's rain.

They hiss.

Wild pig tracks. Pig hunters.

Hannibal's army ran the legions down these mountains, they were surprised, they seized their weapons and clanked down these mountains. To the lake where they were hacked to blood and bones. The massacre took several hours.

How many hours?

What kind of tree, what mountains, how many hours.

9.4 IN AREZZO, TO THE NORTH, three of the four of us would like to view Piero della Francesca's frescoes in the church of San Francesco.

In Arezzo, to the north, three of the four of us find that Piero della Francesca's frescoes in the church of San Francesco are hidden from view for restoration.

In Arezzo, to the north, three of the four of us are walking through the great antiques fair, at which the guidebook sneers.

Up here on the mountain, bare rock and mist and silence.

9.5 PIERO DELLA FRANCESCA'S fresco cycle *The Legend of the True Cross* (1452–66) depicts the discovery of the cross near Jerusalem by Helena, mother of Constantine, and its subsequent adventures.

There are battle scenes ("the chaos of Renaissance warfare"), an Annunciation ("its aura of serenity is typical of Piero's enigmatic style"), and a rendering of the Death of Adam ("illustrates Piero's masterly treatment of anatomy").

Up here on the mountain, wind.

Up here on the mountain, the sun is riding gray surf.

9.6 "WE COULDN'T SEE THEM. Did you see pigs?"

I sit on the stone wall next to the house, gouging mud from the treads of my shoes with kindling.

Place of Blood, Place of Bones.

Mud. Goethe: "Tuscany . . . lies so much lower, the ancient sea has done its duty and piled up a deep loamy soil."

Trees: "Olives . . . look almost like willows . . ."

Cold hard light up on the mountain.

Flashing light—an ambulance?—that inched along the road down in the valley.

9.7 THE FIRE I LIT AND CHOKED ON when I returned.
Eroica hurling itself from Dante's windows.
Baroque sunset.
Hissing logs.
Blood-soaked beach.
Pigs.
Three of the four of us returning from Arezzo.
Curls of mud springing from shoes.
"We couldn't see them."
The clanking running down these mountains, the several hours.
How many hours?

10 THE PHOTOGRAPH IS A PHOTOGRAPH of air. The sun a dot punched through the core of a bruised cloud: swelled to the left, a nauseous gray near the right, overflowing the frame. Part of a mountain at bottom, and small rags of blue among the clouds. You might imagine the entire sky revolving on the pin of the sun, revealing now serenity, now rage.

II WALK THE BANK, PICK A BRIDGE, cross, walk the other bank, pick another bridge. Ponte P. Nenni, Ponte Regina Margherita, Ponte Cavour, Ponte Umberto, Ponte S. Angelo, Ponte Vittorio Eman. II, Ponte Princ. Amedeo, Ponte G. Mazzini, Ponte Sisto, Ponte Garibaldi—one has one's choice. A map compresses some of the longer names to fit each into its river. This, we find, makes us frantic: shards of a script unfathomed from the start.

12.1 WALK UP PAST LUNGOTEVERE AVENTINO past the Cloaca Maxima (Rome's ancient sewer) and the lone remaining arch of a ruined bridge. Cross to Tiber Island by Ponte Fabricio (constructed in 62 B.C.), from which you may enjoy a fine view up and down the river. *In the ancient days* the Romans sculpted the island to lend it resemblance to a ship.

12.2 CROSS FROM TIBER ISLAND to the west bank by Ponte Cestio. Walk up Lungotevere Anguillara, then cross to the east bank by Ponte Garibaldi. Walk up Lungotevere dei Vallati, then cross to the west bank by Ponte Sisto. Walk up Lungotevere d. Farnesina, then cross to the east bank by Ponte G. Mazzini. Walk up Lungotevere d. Sangallo, then cross to the west bank by Ponte Princ. Amedeo. Walk up Lungotevere in Sassia, then cross to the east bank by Ponte Vittorio Eman. II. Walk up Lungotevere degli Altoviti, then cross to the west bank by Ponte S. Angelo. Walk up Lungotevere Castello, then cross to the east bank at Ponte Umberto. Walk up Lungotevere Marzio, then cross to the west bank at Ponte Cavour. Walk up Lungotevere dei Mellini, then cross to the east bank at Ponte Regina Margherita. Walk up Lungotevere Arnaldo da Brescia, then cross to the west bank at Ponte P. Nenni. . . .

12.3 "WELL THEN, TOMORROW EVENING Rome!": or so we said ourselves, two days ago. Now the City hives at us, each Tiber bank hurling its squatness at the sky.

This afternoon through the window of the room where Keats died: the tourist tumult on Piazza di Spagna, where his furniture and doors were burned; palms on rooftops; darkening; yellow shop windows; streetlights winking on.

13 11:30 P.M. AN ENORMOUS TOURING group stands on the Piazza Navona, watching Bernini's fish-men tooting water from ornaments, pigeons grumbling on their heads. Somewhere, bells. A cruiser glides by, low to the stones, every few minutes; U.S. Marines stride stiffly around. Inside the café, a haughty barista wears a dollop of coffee foam on his nose.

A hotel. Rhombus of quivering light. Outside, voices, footsteps, low laughs. Further off, mopeds.

14 THE PHOTOGRAPH IS A PHOTOGRAPH of light. Gold spills over the roofs, a water tower, soft piled hills, roads scratched into land. A huge cypress at the right of the frame, and cars on the City wall.

Clouds. At the left of the frame, birds standing on long shadows on a church; a dagger topping the dome in silhouette. Between the church and the tree, you, looking down over the wall.

15 FROM THE TOP OF THE TOWER, Siena is all fog and terra cotta. There, off to the left, the striped cathedral pokes itself up from a cloud, stone beasties launching and spitting from the spires.

16 THE PHOTOGRAPH IS A PHOTOGRAPH of darkness. Flowers on a small tree; at upper left, a ridge seeps into indigo sky. A utility line crossing from left; and is that the castle jutting behind it, behind the trees? 10:45 P.M. Signs swerve from the dark and vanish. Once familiar; once alien. Lightless nameless terrain. A roadside figure in silhouette.

17 THE PHOTOGRAPH IS A PHOTOGRAPH of land. The valley topped with fog, skimmed out at the house's elevation, like you could stand on it. Around it, the ridge; above, three frame inches of blue sky. It is remarkably like the view from a plane.

At lower left, you, in silhouette, looking at once out and back; on land and in air; displacing.

18 THE PHOTOGRAPH IS A PHOTOGRAPH of travel. Impossible light pours down into the sliced gourd of a tomb; behind it, ordinary trees. Inside, you are approaching.

19 THE PHOTOGRAPH IS A PHOTOGRAPH of writing. You are standing in the Caracalla Baths, the map in one hand, a sign reading APODYTERIUM at left. Up to your neck in a mosaic. Behind you, scarred and pitted stone; in the center of what was once a bustling room, an aperture of sky. And there, when you look closer, a tiny fringe of leaves, along the crumbling sill: the tops of trees.

Notes

EPIGRAPH
The translation is Edmund Jephcott's, from Walter Benjamin, "A Berlin Chronicle" (*Reflections*, Schocken, 1978).

BROADWAY
Quotations and paraphrasings from Walter Benjamin, "Marseille," trans. Edmund Jephcott (*Reflections*, Schocken, 1978); Stephen Jenkins, *The Greatest Street in the World* (G. P. Putnam's Sons, 1911); Susan Edmiston, *Literary New York: A History and Guide* (Houghton Mifflin, 1976). Other works consulted: Pamela Jones, *Under the City Streets* (Holt, Rinehart and Winston, 1938); Charles Lockwood, *Manhattan Moves Uptown: An Illustrated History* (Houghton Mifflin, 1976); James Trager, *West of Fifth: The Rise and Fall and Rise of Manhattan's West Side* (Atheneum, 1987); Rem Koolhaas, *Delirious New York: A Retroactive Manifesto for Manhattan* (Monacelli Press, 1994). Thanks to Franz Peter Hugdahl for pointing me to this last work.

TEXT ON THE WEATHER
Passages and phrasings in "TERMINOLOGY," "AXIOMS; POSSIBLE OR PROBABLE SLOGANS," and "INTERVIEW WITH THE SUCCESSFUL WEATHER-MAN" from John Ciardi, *A Browser's Dictionary: A Compendium of Curious Expressions and Interesting Facts* (Harper and Row, 1980); and *The National Audubon Society Field Guide to North American Weather* (Knopf, 1997).

LOVE IS THREE THINGS

Passages and phrasings from Gerald G. Jampolsky, *Love Is Letting Go of Fear* (Celestial Arts, 1988). "Bilden die Nächte sich nicht . . ." is from a fragment included in John J. L. Mood's *Rilke on Love and Other Difficulties* (Norton, 1975); this translation is my own. "The Three Great Secrets of Birdwatching" is from Edward W. Cronin Jr., *Getting Started in Birdwatching* (Houghton Mifflin, 1996). Frank Hardy's rooftop exploits are chronicled in *Hunting for Hidden Gold* (Grosset and Dunlap, 1975).

NINETEEN ITALIAN DAYS

Quotations and paraphrasings from *The Autobiography of Benvenuto Cellini* (Quality Paperback Book Club, 1995); Goethe, *Italian Journey*, trans. Robert R. Heitner (Suhrkamp, 1989); *Rome* (Eyewitness Travel Guides, 1995); and *Florence and Tuscany* (Eyewitness Travel Guides, 1995).

CITY is for those whose friendship has been the most exhilarant piracy of all.

CPSIA information can be obtained at www.ICGtesting.com
Printed in the USA
LVOW041507050113

314443LV00001B/24/P